HERE

Bobby Byrd

NORTH ATLANTIC BOOKS

ISBN 0-913028-37-1

Publisher's Address:

North Atlantic Books
Route 2, Box 135
Creamery Road
Plainfield, Vermont 05667

Principal Distributor:

Book People
2940 Seventh Street
Berkeley, California 94710

Acknowledgement is made to: *Coyote's Journal, Io, Stooge, Fervent Valley, Goat's Foot, Puerto del Sol, Grosseteste Review, Desert Review, Sailing and Road Clear,* and *Truck* where some of these poems appeared originally.

Cover Drawing by Jane Catherwood Sprague

The text was set in Aldine Roman, an adaptation of the typeface designed by Aldus Manutius in the 15th Century. Composed on the IBM Composer by Typographics, R.D. 2, Plainfield, Vermont.

NOTE

Jim Christy is a friend of mind, teaches me how
to build a house, comes from America, moving off
a farm in Ohio toward the west, the same reasons
such a son of that land moved toward the Pacific
one-hundred years ago. Only Jim knows his motors,
the ways his six-cylinder Ford pick-up runs with
100,000 miles on it, his eyes turned from the gods
and ghosts wandering in these ancient volcanic
mountains, the San Juans. These poems are for Jim,
a blessing for the land, the dreams up North
Carnero Creek.

the breath

what happens / must happen
            over and over again.
knowing comes
in like way, the way
            water moves, the earth
and the sun, darkness
            and light (not so easy
to understand if you
            use your head): the sun
   blinds the eyes
            until shadow, the black
            of timber and heavy smell
(cow elk jumps into the sun
            falling red
            behind mountains, a crow
            whips its wings,
            the sun gone
and a cold breeze blows
            toward the first stars
            rising.

monday afternoon

tired brain goes
the way of the wind
bringer of rain
down from timberline.
    (quiet day
grey clouds in a single
place of america
                  lost
place unknown of
"the united states"
so I make songs
for my unborn child:

       I will sleep now
       and dream while
       the wild roses bloom.

THE FIRST OF JUNE

Tonight the clouds bringing rain haze the
waxing moon now into June in these high
mountains and Lee my woman tells me about
the garden she plants: four kinds of let-
tuce, two of beans, red and white potatos,
beets, turnips, cucumbers, spinach, swiss
chard, sweet peas, marigolds, poppies,
zinnias. Above us where the water runs
through the dark mountains the red colum-
bines and wild strawberries are in bloom.
I remember last night's dream: a black
woman taught me about Isis, told me the
cunt of the Goddess is of jewels. The rain
falls now, and beyond the black clouds are
stars, and moon.

CHANGES

Heaven in the Mountain:
summer solstice comes and
my woman sleeps with baby
and a June rain fell
(the stars came out) —
and I don't know, and so
it goes, and so it goes.

Note on Omens: July, 1971

Two days ago in a heavy July rain we saw a
deer running back and forth across a field of
freshly cut hay next to our house. We were
pulling out on the highway at the time, and
at the edge of the field in the high uncut
grass we saw a fawn, its leg caught in the woven
wire fence. I stopped the car and ran through
the wet grass, but by the time I reached the fawn,
the leg was free. The doe watched from the other
side of the field. The fawn did not move, but shook
from fear, my smell, her wild black eyes still, the
spotted coat hanging with dampness. I turned back
to the car. Today, talking with the foreman of the
ranch, I asked him if he had seen the fawn. He said
yes, said his labrador bitch had run it down that
morning in the clump of cottonwoods by the river.
The dog had broken the fawn's neck.

Death is too simple (natural) of an event, or se-
quence of events, not to have motion beyond the body
of that fawn. I remember the fawn's eyes, the rain,
the smell of cut grass: such things happen around me,
and I feel them, their occurrence somehow energy with-
in my life, not necessarily as omen, but at least as
current through the darkness of my dreams. I do not
say I understand any intended meaning. I say such
death, and life too, occurs around me, and that it
does have meaning. It is the way an angel might
speak. It is like the *I-Ching*: the yarrow stalks
are not mine, but they do fall from my fingers. I
live among these mountains. I am part of the same
law.

— in memory of
Striker Wonder

POLITICAL POEM
— for Steve

the seasons pass.
mountain winter comes
& my wife with child
unknowing in dark belly
knows constant love.
we will die . . .

                  revolution is
                  this circle —
a dance round &
round about a fire
Willow Creek flowing
the changes of the moon.

this morning I drowned
a dying grey kitten
in the irrigation ditch.
afterwards I picked the last of
the sweet clover, the wild
grasses and flowers
for our breakfast table.
kneeling at the water
I prayed for the dead cat,
& now I make this poem
in celebration of all that.

SEPTEMBER

in the briar patch
we picked rosehips
for our winter supply
of Vitamin-C.
coming back home
the sun setting
an old cow moaning
my woman she sung
we gather together
to ask the Lord's blessings.

for the love of God
I took a pee
doing a dance
in the dust.
I get wet the same way
when I'm drunk.

the last of summer

and somebody said
to the old man
(El Viejo) that
it looked like
rain goddamn

and he said
it might
but it won't
(laughing)

and the grey skies
broke blue
and my daughter ate
wild raspberries
from the bushes
while she danced.

    — for Jose Atencio

SATURDAY NIGHT

with Joel Oppenheimer
I'll sing for Li Po
jumped in the dark
flowing water / drunk
to fuck the moon
(wise yellow legs)
& come up red roses
the likes of which
you never smelled.
by god me too got drunk
stumbling beneath the stars
but my world still holds
together, defiantly.
the moon gets full
& rests in the flesh
of these bony mountains.
I'll be the next in line.

THE AMCHITKA BLAST

I pack Susannah
(sleeping)
on my back
up Shaw Creek.
Migrating robins
dig for food
in dry leaves
of the quakies,
make noise like
startled deer.
The fools who rule us
will never learn
to sing, nor make
such noise.
That is simple
enough: they offer
death for their
fat idea of America
and I offer this
with no facts,
nor flourish,
                but

my baby rides
on my back (sleeping)
and the creek falls
from the mountain
and there's a hawk
in the blue sky.
I will make a prayer
for this round earth.
My daughter will dance!
We go up / weaving
on game trails,
the sun bright
on patches of snow.

August

sunflowers
dead bugs
summertime
woman
black hole
new moon
and death

THE SOUTH FORK DUMP

"There aint no
flies on Jesus,"
an old song says,
August flies buzzing
all round my head.
"Bullshit!" says I
smiling in the stink
after killing five
in one quick swat.
I watch the crows,
the magpies, the jays:
they know where its at
in all this shit.
Caw / Caw / Caw
they sing, eating
leftover steak, or
pecking at the skull
of a bloated cow.
They bless this place
by dancing in the sun.
They take. They eat.
Caw / Caw / Caw.
In remembrance of us all.

— for Ted Barrow

notions for politics

the idea is
to take a shit
in the right place
smiling for your
own salvation
if you want
to get it going

america / ^{via} without
benjamin franklin or
the united states.
but I'm talking too much
for thursday afternoon.
I hardly know the news
no more
          — drinking booze
and watching the snow
come from the east
the place of / the sun
and the month's new moon.

STATEMENT

its been a long day
loading adobe bricks
for our house of earth
and wood for the roof.
now the sun goes down
and a new moon follows.
the coming stars are dim
are gone

      in the city .
there the moon
is found by chance —
I want to go back
my drunk and sadtime
sometime bastard dream.
the yellow piss breaks
the crust of snow.
tomorrow we'll make money
to keep our bellies full.

wednesday morning game
— for Douglas Merrill

6 magpies sit
on the top fence rail.
watching 1 grey cat.
the 3 of us (eating
2 pancakes each)
watch the 6 magpies
while the 1 cat takes
a running quick shit
among infinite grass.

    so be it!

the game ends in a tie.

north carnero creek
—for Jim

toilet paper
in hand I dug
like mad
in the rocks
and above me
I discovered
bright red Mars
planet of Aries
in the cloudy sky.
I emptied myself.
afterwards I drank
from the creek
laying on my belly,
and the august night
smelled of winter
smelled of sage
and my woman slept
with our baby
and Mars (planet of
my birth) wandered
with the wind
across the night.

down by the riverside

down by the riverside
among the green grasses
I just saw a mushroom

        sprouting — O
        let's go to bed
        & make summer love.

BIRTH-MONTH
— **for Tyana Rye Josselyn America**

above Willow Creek
flies buzzing
sun off
a hawk's wings
circling, circling
where rabbits die

its August:
the does and fawns
stay up high
above these flies,
but the bucks
they come down
belly cool at midday
in the black earth
of aspen groves.

here the wind knows
the land, the hawk
knows the wind.
we are here
to do what we can.

THE NEWS

and now I'm told
Queen Bees
aren't hatching

and drones
won't carry summer
between their legs

and fools
from Hell walk on
the August moon.

TIRED

Tonight after all of our friends left — I split wood,
whap-whap-whap, for two hours, wood for the cooking
fire, wood to keep us warm. The energy flowed from
me, nervous from the people, from not being able to
say anything to those who are my friends. I avoid it,
hide from it, piss on the stones and trees, the markers
of my ego. The poet. The Poet. But I cannot speak,
form the words, the right ritual, give thanks!

*The gods, the gods! The lady rides the moon! She
wears the mask of death, the light of the southward
moving sun.*

What do I say? Crack the nut, let the seed open, let
what may / flower — that's what I should be about,
give myself at least that chance, the chance that this
winter, these nights below zero, the clear skies, the
Pliedes in the east window, may be a spring of sorts,
twitching of unknown greenery, roots taking hold.
Nothing is real anyway. I can light a fire with this
paper, the wood. Whap-whap-whap. Ice chokes the river.
Nothing moves. I'm tired. And the animals in the
mountains sleep, sleep.

WHAT HAPPENS IN SANTA FE
— for Diana's garden

At Santa Fe drunk and stoned
and as always
in that summer heat
awoke hungover and this time
with a baby between us,
a goddamn rooster crowing
hot sun in the truck.

I remember that morning
squash blossoms and beets.
There were too many
people to tell it too,
and on the way back home
we drank a beer in Ojo Caliente
and made love standing up.

RITES

Paul Blackburn is dead. And today the first snow
came, came early. Its late night, and I drink my
red wine, the cold falling from the mountains, as
always, following a snow in the clear sky. I did
what was needed, picked some lettuce, the parsley,
the flowers — stood out there in the cold, my fingers
numb, getting all that done. Winter comes quickly
now: I want to get drunk, this world turning, spinning
black mother of my dreams. The Rio Grande flows
south, runs summer home through the light of these
stars. Tomorrow I will bring down dry aspen and
pine for the cold night fires to keep us warm.

The Latrine

on the bluff above
ice-running South Fork
ponderosa pine
quiet wind in the snow / cold
high winter and fire-made
slake old mountains

the rough slats
frozen piss seat and the drop
8 foot into she-earth
before I'm done.

            – for Ruth & Jim

HUNTING ABOVE SHAW CREEK

Today I borrowed a .22 single shot, went rabbit
hunting up above Shaw Creek, and there on the
ridge in the pinyon, I shot a rabbit, and he did
not die, and I hit him in the skull with the
rifle butt, and sat down in the snow, skinned and
cleaned him, left his guts and head there in the
bloody snow for coyote. I killed him for meat.
I killed him in order to learn how to kill. I
gave prayer to the rabbit, and went on up the
hill, carrying his carcass in a plastic bag.

*

in the sky is a waning moon.
days get longer.
I walk in the mountains
quietly with rabbit ghost
meat for my belly.
the pinyon crackle
like fire in the wind
and rabbit teaches of death,
pulling off fur in wintertime,
vapor rising in cold air,
dead meat on bones, open eyes.
I'll kill me another rabbit.
he'll bless me with his life.

HERE

this October night
the gold of aspen trees
a dream in moonless black
while the water keeps
coming down .

                  climbing
the grey rock ridge / 3 crows
watch me from the sun
flying with the wind
        this turning
this breathing, the sweet
      black hands of Kali, Jesus-
              lover

*

the flowers are dead
and the water flows
and flows from the mountain.
dreaming, my woman
sleeps next to me,
        tits and cunt,
belly heavy for birth
full with my seed
to flower in the winter sun
and on this frozen earth.

night poem for the lady
                — north carnero creek
                november, 1970

darkness is the light
in darkness, clear water
moves beneath the ice.
these mountains
like a woman's thighs
at the edge of stars
are a history of fire,
of water, of wind:
                the earth
turns and the white moon
is full in cold night
(my bones, brittle as death),
flames rising from the fire.

a november tale
— for Paul Malanga

snow on the ground,
half-moon just gone,
my piss steaming,
I heard
          the splayed hooves
of a single buck
          clatter up the rock
                    toward

the horns of taurus
the hands of gemini
and the deep black cunt
of the great she-bear.

song

under the moon sky
bright six inches
of snow we walk
my bellied woman
one month away and I
talk of dead hero lost
dreaming Jack Kerouac
tracks of coyote jesus
loves sweet baby and this
is no cold winter blues.

OKAY THEN.

Here it goes — like the deer tracks I saw today in
the fresh snow, meandering over a small mesa from
bush to clump of grass to bush. They were taking
it easy (the hunters gone back to the city), feeding
where the chance provided, eyes and ears alert, but
a good day it was beneath the low clouds, high-
stepping through the snow. That's what it should
be with a poem. But then, goddamnit, its not that
easy, don't say nothing about the wild black eyes
of the deer, trail knowledge, hoof sure, or the
head of a big buck, 5 points, dripping blood, his
tongue sticking out, shot by a woman from a car —
quick photo behind the head, twitching her ass,
forgot it all in a week, except in her dreams. The
buck, that one, is dead. But then, there's his
seed in the belly of a doe, walking the mountains,
waiting for spring.

MEMO (11/23/70)

there aint no place to go.
there aint nothing to do.
its a cold night with stars.
it all gets done.
the willow leaves are gone.

NOVEMBER

splitting wood
in a cold wind
got me tired,

& now the night
got me drinking.
on the wall

are photographs
of three women,
two dead poets.

I write in my
journal of dreams,
hexagrams, symbols,

& all the while
the earth she
turns again toward

the rising sun.
but I aint saying
I got need to worry.

my woman sleeps
in a warm bed.
there's wood for

the cooking fire,
& for a poet's luck,
there's a skunk

sleeps the winter
beneath my house.

BULLS

this morning the snow falls
gently at my feet, and the bulls
in the pasture paw for grass
unconcerned, their great backs
covered white like the mountains.
they got their's this summer.
and I? well, I made love
last night, fine good love
in the darkness with my lady
after trying too hard
to write a poem, to make
some meaning out of this life
I call my own, and this morning
with chores to do, well shit!
I'm happy to let the snow fall
gently, gently / at my feet.

THANKSGIVING, 1970

The snow came in
the morning. No sun
for our Thanksgiving.
I had a flat tire.
We had to work
for the money.
Now we will eat.
I will get drunk.
But before I do
I will give these
mountains, this snow,
the sun, the moon,
to our child who grows
in your womb, dreaming,
him or her, whomever
our love has made.

PLACE

1.
The snow falls.
The moon is lost.
And the sun
is the other world,
the light of which
I seek. People
wander in my head.
God's mouth is closed.
And my father smiles
from a photograph,
stinks of death,
pilot of a plane
burning,
          the bright
flames licking
damp Mississippi skies.
I was two years old.

2.
Who am I? Where
a woman to bear me a son?
I want no more
of dreams, nor of
darkness — only light,
that of the winter sun
and its secret of plants,
the sage and chamisa:
life hung in the roots
in the frozen earth.
the bones of my worlds
are breaking (money spent),
days and years: I will die.
I am the man my father was.
I will be who I am.

TIME OF GOOD HOPE

and Jesus clad
in a man's flesh
making magic
before old men.

Somewhere I said / there aint nothing to say. So
we get stronger in the process. Anyway a man gets
at a poem, open it up for the eating, share its
flesh, its seed, its rind, then goddamn, get it
done. Even if there is nothing to say. Who are
we to warrant miracles more than the deer, camp-
robbers, jays, bears, loggers, etc. in the mountains
as winter solstice comes round, Jesus being born
beside the Angel Death, my woman singing carols to
our baby. I don't know why: I want to scream. Dig
a hole in the snow, I tell myself, find the actual
darkness, sing to the mother death, find the sun
again, head between the legs, black, black, then
the light of the sun, eating fat trout in the spring,
muddy waters, dreams, days go by, green leaves,
green . . .

THE RABBIT

the snowshoe
rabbit, his
white body and
eyes black
in the snow,
eats brown grass,
dead leaves.
you can sing
and he dont move.
he knows the winter
was never the end.
the bobcat is
his brother, with
sure green eyes, quick
paws and a belly
for meat. he knows too.
now you know.

     — for my daughter

december

the snow falls gently
and magpie sleeps.
dawn will bring him
bones and fresh meat.

THE NEW YEAR COMES

And the earth moves round
And I'll wait near the place of the hole
Where the spring comes out of the mountain
the mud heavy with moss and flowering weeds.

       – for Jane

Winter Prose

Two pairs of socks. Long underwear. Bluejeans from
Penny's. Wool shirt. Quilted shirt. Bluejean coat.
Pullover wool hat. Wool gloves. Leather mittens.
Enough to keep any man warm these winter mornings.
Keep your toes moving. But my hands get numb, ache
until I get something done. I get lazy in winter,
write short poems, sleep much, spend time sick, wait
for visions in sleep, drink too much, expend energy
changing my life, split and cut wood, read the *I-Ching*,
fuck my wife, go for walks, watch the baby, sing songs,
go slow, go slow, think about bears and racoons, wander
through books, stoke the fire, write letters, wait
for letters, work only some for a living, dream in the
daytime, keep warm, keep my family warm, watch the
river, the ice, watch the deer and stray cats, watch
the jays, magpies, blackbirds, juncoes, chickadees,
camprobbers, a very few robins, watch the sun and the
moon. watch the stars, stay inside, watch football
games, talk with friends, drink with friends, watch
the weather, talk about the weather, worry about my
poetry, work at it, feed the cats, feed the goats in
the morning, start the car, feed the goats in the
evening, put up the car, eat breakfast, lunch and
dinner, keep fat in my belly, learn what I can (never
can speak it), spend time hating and loving, want to
change it all, want my sadness and agony, want what-
ever happiness, want the winter cold, want my woman,
want the house warm, want the want to know myself,
want my fear, my darkness, my songs . . . Susannah
is crying for warm milk and only her mother can give
it to her. In the black window the waning moon is
rising. Where do I go from here?

MEMO #2 (12/71)

Be aware of death until
You know what death is.
In the spring Old Woman Wind
Will blow these mountains dry.

the light of the moon

tracks of rabbit
two coyote
in the light of
a quarter moon.
we wait for a
child, the birth of
eyes from darkness.
the creek is ice.
black mountains around us
were born of fire.

35 BELOW ZERO

goddamn so cold
its the heart
of a woman (skunk-
pussy / elk-cunt,
belly of stars)
walking quietly
and waiting.

during Capricorn

The darkness. The light. An Aries walks on the
ridge between the two, I am told, feels the strain
of each, the sun balanced there, for a time, as the
year turns toward the spring. But now it is winter,
only two weeks after the solstice, and the days,
slowly, get longer. A man I know asks for facts,
and it is to the sun I turn him — there is the fact,
the light, and its mirror, the moon, male and female.
Then to the stars. To the earth. The plants. The
animals. Facts. Wandering beasts in the imagination.
Women and men. Children. The fetus dreaming in the
dark liquid of innocence, of total sweet pleasure.
Where do we go? The politicians tell very dull tales,
babble of power, protection, economics, and finally
of God — they keep their night dreams hidden, the
secrets of their genitals, sluggish sceptres and
holes of their egos, goddamned death swinging back
and forth before their eyes. Where do we go? The
poet is a dead man. He offers form with words, a
dance lost so long ago he grasps for it, stretches
out fingers, asks for miracles of God's doom and
resurrection. Says he is power. Music. Words.
Knowing. Its said he don't create a thing, and
that's a fact. Where do we go? On the doorstep
a starveling cat whines, whines, whines, and I gave
him some food, but won't let him in. The winter is
around him. As is death. As is spring. Life, all
things, turn round. I can say this, but still I am
afraid. I am afraid. I walk on that ridge: the
darkness, the light.

THE THAW
— the rock
above Lost Lake

in the January sun
the chinook, the rock,
the winds, an old Ute
holy place, a place
to watch the sun enter the mountains,
the earth spinning toward night,
the stars, the dawn,
and there is no end —

                *

        I sat on my pants, naked
        bones and flesh, the blue sky,
        making song and prayer
        for the light of the sun.
        I am not ready for spring.

song of february

belly sick from
drunk, dead tired,
pissed at the world,
the united states of
the sunday paper —
while up Willow Creek
in a sun-bright aspen grove
the antlers of a bull elk
fall to the ground.
the year changes, now.

NOTES (2/22/71)

in these mountains, the San Juans
the snow the wind the grey clouds
and inside this house
the baby cries, cunt
being cleaned by her mother
and me her father sits
thinks what happens with words
his daughter's cunt, his wife
mother with a baby of one week
mother who gave birth, gives child
during the calving season
the calves dropping
like the baby Susannah
with a change
in barometric pressure
and a friend who said
how nice
we are so attached

the way
the baby's head
comes from between her mother's thighs
from full belly and the light
of darkness
purple with mucous and blood
crying with grey eyes wide open
the shock of first light
and her mother laughing
its a girl!
still attached by cord
by blood the love
has been the body
yes the pain the breath
and the man watches
his mouth a hole for words
will enter the body

later
when his time comes
his seed the sun
the wind the water the earth:
it has been so
since Susannah's birth
the calves from the cows
still dropping.

THE MIRACLE

Tomorrow night is the dark of the moon. I
get drunk, drinking whisky slowly. The night
is warm — sadness of no spring, melting snows,
storm climbing between us and the stars, the
bright Dog Star, the falling Venus. I do not
know myself, not even the simplest motions of
my body. Tonight I am fat with the bread my
woman made. Tomorrow I am thin with the breath
the mountains give me, my arms, my hands, my
eyes. To be sane, to be whole — nothing is
promised with life, with human life, mere scales
between sun and moon. I take the easy way so
many times, the search ending in a book, the
Bible, the Coyote Myth, the Teachings of Don
Juan, anything, any/way, wholeness looked for,
but cheaply, cheaply. I get drunk, Which way,
which hole, which mountain, which stream? I
want to tell a story, but what story? And my
daughter Susannah watches me from her enormous
brown eyes, does not "care" for me, does not
"love" me, but is at times joyous with me, angry
with me, and it all passes, from each second on-
ward, each second *now*, at this instant, the baby
holding to my legs, laughing or crying, now, now,
now, now, now, now — I do not know what she knows,
eyes of my baby, joyous eyes, brown eyes, one
year old this week, my seed in her body, my seed
born from her mother, the sun and the earth, the
spring and the fall. I repeat: I want to tell a
story, but what story? Tomorrow night is the
dark of the moon.

Poem

wind blows thunder
from where
the sun rises.
I want to know of
Gods (goddamn them)
wandering quiet
in the mountains.
my feet make noise.
three deer scatter,
their dark bellies
carrying birth
for mountain spring.

Harbinger

heavy balls,
fat robins
mud and
wet socks.

I watch my
woman's ass
and our baby cries.

DAILY BREAD

the last winter moon
wanes in mountain sky.
and spring comes, a time
for planting of seed, I sing:
the world lives on death.
we will eat. we will die.
I drink wine, get drunk,
while in the other room
baby Susannah sucks
from her mother's tits.
she lives! goddamn —
I should learn so much!

MAKING MONEY

In January the rich man I work for shot a
stray cat outside his door with a .22 pis-
tol. It was a poor shot, and the cat, drag-
ging its rear legs through the snow, was
able to struggle to the very center of the
frozen river. There the body now lays,
untouched by any scavenger — tracks of coyotes,
wing marks of a hawk, others, have scarred the
snow around the cat's body, but none have
eaten of that carrion. The man has pointed
out the cat to his friends, saying with humor
that it would keep until spring. He was right.
There it has been for two months, the suns,
the moons, crossing it each day. Three snows
have melted from around it. Now the first
warm winds of spring blow down from the moun-
tains. The last winter moon wanes. And soon
the ice will break, giving the spring river,
rising muddy and warm, the blessing of those
bones. Nothing has been gained. The man is
no animal master, this no sacrificial hunt.
Across the river in the fields the crows eat
the last of the winter dead.

WOOD

hands, an axe, dry aspen
WHACK   WHACK   WHACK
to make time with
& fire for food, bones
in the hands for a woman (Ruth
to hold after such dance
making heat

a fire from bones
like all women should
here in the San Juans
"on the back of this beast" America
the aspen sprung green
from today's sweet rain.

                    — for Jim

DRINKING ROUND A FIRE

being bone tired
not quite drunk
I can't even think
shit from shinola
and with friend John
(who asks nothing)
I drink more red wine,
dreaming sweet pussy
in these deep mountains,
dark flowers sprouting
from the warm shit
of such a cold spring.

ALL SONGS ARE FOR DEATH

1.
Dead aspen tree hole
where woodpecker lived
burns quick and hot,
makes the darkness warm.
I sit by the creek,
night running the wind
through the flutes of
these mountains, me
scratching my nuts, me
waiting for spring.

2.
camprobber with his wing
busted (his magic)
can't sit at the top
of the holy blue spruce.
I cannot shoot him.
he dies by the water.
the mountains are gone.

3.
riding the circle
of the sacred snake
the snow melting
the warm winds
muddy waters, and
I come home to my
sacred snatch: now
she sings to a child.

THE JOURNEY

It will be a man
who leads the way.
The earth, she

circles the sun.
But now I know of
nothing, except

the summer rain
falling in this
very dry year.